Faithful

I found *Faithful* to be a gripping, vividly illustrated examination of God's faithfulness throughout the Bible: rigorous in its theology, yet accessible to me as an everyday Christian. By the end of the thirty days, I felt challenged to greater faithfulness – not when life might improve but, right now, in my place of struggle.

Sharon Hastings, doctor and author of Wrestling with My Thoughts

We need to know and experience the faithfulness of God in these troubled times, when all seems to be so uncertain. These devotions drawn from the Bible will help us to know better the faithful and eternal God we serve, and to trust more strongly in him.

Jeremy Marshall, former CEO of the UK's oldest private bank,
C. Hoare & Co., Chairman of Christianity Explored and author
of Beyond the Big C

30-DAY DEVOTIONAL

Faithful

Edited by Elizabeth McQuoid

INTER-VARSITY PRESS
36 Causton Street, London SW1P 4ST, England
Email: ivp@ivpbooks.com
Website: www.ivpbooks.com

First published 2021

British Library Cataloguing-in-Publication Data
A catalogue record for this book is available from the British Library.

ISBN: 978–1–78974–341–8
eBook ISBN: 978–1–78974–342–5

Set in Avenir 11/15pt
Typeset in Great Britain by CRB Associates, Potterhanworth, Lincolnshire
Printed in Great Britain by Ashford Colour Press Ltd, Gosport, Hampshire

Produced on paper from sustainable sources.

Inter-Varsity Press publishes Christian books that are true to the Bible and that communicate the gospel, develop discipleship and strengthen the church for its mission in the world.

IVP originated within the Inter-Varsity Fellowship, now the Universities and Colleges Christian Fellowship, a student movement connecting Christian Unions in universities and colleges throughout Great Britain, and a member movement of the International Fellowship of Evangelical Students. Website: www.uccf.org.uk. That historic association is maintained, and all senior IVP staff and committee members subscribe to the UCCF Basis of Faith.

Contributors

Genesis 15:1–21 and Revelation 2:18–29
Tim Chester
Tim is a faculty member of Crosslands Training, a former chair of Keswick Ministries and the author or co-author of more than forty books. He was previously Research and Policy Director for Tearfund UK.

1 Samuel 13:5–14
Peter Maiden
Peter was International Director of Operation Mobilisation and later became International Director Emeritus. He served Keswick Ministries as Minister-at-Large and also wrote a number of books, including *Discipleship Matters: Dying to live for Christ* and *Radical Gratitude: Recalibrating your heart in an age of entitlement*.

Psalm 119:97–104
Alistair Begg
Alistair has been the Senior Pastor at Parkside Church, Cleveland, Ohio, USA, since 1983. He has written a number of books, including *Pray Big*. A popular conference

speaker, he is also the voice behind the daily radio broad-cast *Truth for Life.*

Acts 20:17–38
Jonathan Lamb
Jonathan is Minister-at-Large for Keswick Ministries. He previously worked as CEO of Keswick Ministries and as Director of Langham Preaching, and had leadership roles in IFES (International Fellowship of Evangelical Students) and UCCF (Universities and Colleges Christian Fellowship). He is the author of a number of books, including *Integrity: Leading with God watching* and *Preaching Matters: Encountering the living God.*

1 Thessalonians 2:1–12
Malcolm Duncan
Malcolm is Lead Pastor at Dundonald Elim Church, Belfast. In addition to being Chair of Elim's Ethics and Public Theology Task Force, he is also Theologian-in-Residence for Spring Harvest and Essential Christian, and the author of a number of books.

1 Thessalonians 5:1–28
Alec Motyer
Alec was Vice Principal of Clifton Theological College, Bristol, and Vicar of St Luke's Church, Hampstead, before

becoming Principal of Trinity College, Bristol. He was much loved on both sides of the Atlantic as a Bible expositor and a prolific author.

2 Timothy 4:1–22 and Hebrews 3:1 – 5:6
Michael Baughen

Michael served as Rector of Holy Trinity Church, Platt Lane, Rusholme, Manchester, and at All Souls, Langham Place in London, before becoming the Bishop of Chester. Following his retirement, he worked as an honorary assistant bishop in the dioceses of London and Southwark. He is also a hymn writer.

2 Timothy 4:9–10
Sinclair Ferguson

Sinclair is a teaching fellow and Professor of Systematic Theology at Reformed Theological Seminary, USA, commuting from Scotland, where he is an assistant minister at St Peter's Free Church of Scotland, Dundee. He previously taught at Westminster Theological Seminary, Philadelphia, USA, and was a pastor at First Presbyterian Church, Columbia, South Carolina, and St George's Tron Church, Glasgow. He is the author of numerous books.

Hebrews 6:11–20
Tom Putt

Tom is Vicar of St John the Baptist, Burford, Oxfordshire. Previously, he served as Associate Minister at St John's and St Andrew's in Yeovil, Somerset. He is involved in leading the children's ministry at the Keswick Convention.

Preface

What is the collective name for a group of preachers? A troop, a gaggle, a chatter, a pod . . . ? I'm not sure! But in this Food for the Journey series, we have gathered an excellent group of Bible teachers to help us unpack the Scriptures and understand some of the core issues that every Christian needs to know.

Each book is based on a particular theme and contains excerpts from messages given by much loved Keswick Convention speakers, past and present. When necessary, the language has been updated but, on the whole, this is what you would have heard had you been listening in the tent on Skiddaw Street. A wide, though not exhaustive, selection of Bible passages explores the key theme, and each day of the devotional ends with a fresh section on how to apply God's Word to your own life and situation.

Whether you are a Convention regular or have never been to Keswick, this Food for the Journey series provides a unique opportunity to study the Scriptures and a particular topic with a range of gifted Bible teachers by your side. Each book is designed to fit in your jacket pocket, rucksack or handbag, so that you can read it anywhere – over the breakfast table, on the commute into work or college, while you are waiting in your car, during your lunch break or in bed at night. Wherever life's journey takes you, time in God's Word is vital nourishment for your spiritual journey.

Our prayer is that these devotionals become your daily feast, a nourishing opportunity to meet with God through his Word. Read, meditate on, apply and pray through the Scriptures for each day, and allow God's truths to take root and transform your life.

If these devotionals whet your appetite for more, there is a 'For further study' section at the end of each book. You can also visit our website <www.keswickministries.org> to find the full range of books, study guides, CDs, DVDs and mp3s available.

Let the word of Christ dwell in you richly.
(Colossians 3:16, ESV)

Introduction
A promise kept

Eight years short of his retirement, Robertson McQuilkin stepped down as President of Columbia Bible College and Seminary to look after his wife Muriel. She was suffering from advanced Alzheimer's disease. His book *A Promise Kept* recounts the joys and struggles they shared as he cared for her at home for thirteen years, until her death in 2003. In his resignation speech, he explained:

> When the time came, the decision was firm. It took no great calculation. It was a matter of integrity. Had I not promised, 42 years before, 'in sickness and in health . . . till death do us part'?
>
> This was no grim duty to which I was stoically resigned, however . . . She had, after all, cared for me for almost four decades with marvelous devotion; now it was my turn. And such a partner she was! If I took care of her for 40 years, I would never be out of her debt.[1]

Of course, we don't all have the emotional and financial resources to look after our loved ones like this. But we are drawn to such loving faithfulness and moved by Robertson

McQuilkin's selfless devotion. Yet his faithfulness to his wife is only a pale reflection of Christ's commitment to his bride, the church. God says to his people:

> I have loved you with an everlasting love;
>   I have drawn you with unfailing kindness.
> (Jeremiah 31:3)

The story of the Bible is of God's relentless faithfulness to his purposes and people. From Genesis onwards, we see that, although sin ruptured the relationship that God enjoyed with his people, he didn't abandon them. Instead, he put his salvation plan into motion. He promised a messiah and put a system of animal sacrifice in place, anticipating a once-and-for-all sacrifice for sin, when his own Son would die in our stead. Throughout the Old Testament, looking forward to that day, God pledged his love and faithfulness to his people in a series of covenants – promises that he not only initiated but also bound himself to keep. He called on the people to respond in obedience but, tragically, Scripture is littered with their failures. In the final covenant, the New Covenant established at Calvary, God did everything that needed to be done; he took our ability to keep the covenant out of the equation. Now Jesus' death would be sufficient for the forgiveness of our sins. His resurrection would be the guarantee of eternal life with God in the new heavens and the new earth, and his ascension the catalyst for God's Spirit to come, renewing our hearts and helping us to keep his commands.

Although the cross was the most powerful demonstration of God's love and faithfulness, it was not the last. Because God is the true God who always tells the truth, what he says, he will also do. Daily, we see his faithfulness in action.

- He hears us when we pray.

- He forgives us when we repent.

- He purifies us as we read and meditate on Scripture.

- He transforms us into the likeness of Christ.

- He keeps our salvation secure and guarantees our eternal destiny.

While God's faithfulness is not in any doubt, we are acutely aware of our own tendency for lukewarm devotion. We have the Holy Spirit enabling our obedience but grace-driven effort is still needed. It doesn't take many days without prayer, Bible reading, Christian service and fellowship before our awareness of God falters, our desire for deepening discipleship lessens and our spiritual fervour takes a nosedive. Great acts of faithlessness and public declarations of unbelief don't usually come 'out of the blue'. More often than not, they are the result of these incremental, almost unnoticeable, steps away from the Lord. The Victorian preacher Charles Spurgeon wisely said:

> No professing Christian falls into the great open sin all at once; much backsliding has gone before. See the tree blown down by the strong winds; nine times out of ten, if you look carefully at it, you will see that insects have been at work at it years before, and rotted it; and, therefore, when at last the trial came, it only consummated [completed] what had long been going on.[2]

How do we stem the tide? The recipe for faithfulness is not glamorous or spectacular. It is a daily decision to 'set your heart[s] . . . set your mind[s]' on Christ (Colossians 3:1–2). It is remembering God's grace and goodness and, with the Holy Spirit's help, obeying his will each day. As the hymn reminds us:

> Oh, to grace how great a debtor
> daily I'm constrained to be!
> Let thy goodness, like a fetter,
> bind my wandering heart to thee:
> prone to wander, Lord, I feel it,
> prone to leave the God I love;
> here's my heart, O take and seal it;
> seal it for thy courts above.[3]

Knowing that we are held in the grip of God's unending faithfulness enables us to be faithful for the long haul, and in the small things too. When ministry is tough and lacking in results, when family life is hard and loved ones are suffering, when finances are stretched and the future is uncertain, God stands with us, strengthening our resolve and cultivating his Spirit of faithfulness within us (2 Thessalonians 3:3; Galatians 5:22).

This 30-day devotional looks at a selected range of Bible passages that introduce us to this theme of God's faithfulness and ours. We look at God's faithfulness to his people and promises (Genesis 15; Hebrews 6); God's Word and Spirit as the means of our faithfulness (Psalm 119); the challenge to live with integrity, being faithful to the gospel publicly and privately (Acts 20; 1 Thessalonians 2; Revelation); the way back to God after failure (1 Samuel; 2 Timothy); how we can guard our wayward hearts (Hebrews 3 – 4); and how our faithfulness and God's work together (1 Thessalonians 5).

This short book is an invitation to delight in the faithfulness of God and, in so doing, grow ever more faithful, trusting in him, his promises and his purpose.

Notes

1 Quoted in Sarah Eekhoff Zylstra, 'Died: Robertson McQuilkin, College President Praised for Alzheimer's Resignation', 2 June 2016, <www.christianitytoday.com/news/2016/june/died-robertson-mcquilkin-columbia-president-alzheimers-ciu.html>, accessed 15 December 2020.

2 C. H. Spurgeon, 'Backsliding Healed', sermon no. 920, 13 March 1870, *The Metropolitan Tabernacle Pulpit Sermons*, vol. 16, Passmore & Alabaster, 1870.

3 Robert Robinson, 'Come, Thou Fount of Every Blessing', 1758.

Genesis

'In the beginning God . . .' The early chapters of Genesis set the scene for the whole Bible, introducing us to an eternal and powerful, yet loving God. As the book traces the story from Adam to Joseph, we discover that God spoke, created and designed us for fellowship with him and with one another. This opening section of the Bible introduces us to a number of firsts – the first individuals, the first sin and the first sacrifice for sin. Even though sin ruptured the relationship between a holy God and his people, he did not abandon them. Rather, he set in motion his eternal plan of redemption, and established covenants pledging his love and faithfulness. As God called his people to obedience, he proved himself to be a God who speaks truth, keeps his promise, and is faithful to his character, purposes and glory.

Day 1

Read Genesis 15:1–21
Key verses: Genesis 15:5–7

....

> ⁵ He [God] took him outside and said, 'Look up at the sky and count the stars – if indeed you can count them.' Then he said to him, 'So shall your offspring be.'
>
> ⁶ Abram believed the Lord, and he credited it to him as righteousness.
>
> ⁷ He also said to him, 'I am the LORD, who brought you out of Ur of the Chaldeans to give you this land to take possession of it.'

Are you good at keeping promises?

God has been keeping – and is still keeping – the promise that he made more than four thousand years ago.

God had commanded Abraham to leave his home (Genesis 12), and now promises him a people and a land (Genesis 15:5 and 7). This promise is not just to Abraham but to his people, to us. In Galatians 3:8, Paul says that, through this promise made to Abraham, God 'announced the gospel in advance'. This promise comes to us in the Lord Jesus Christ. As Paul says, 'If you belong to Christ, then you are Abraham's seed, and heirs according to the promise' (Galatians 3:29). And so, in Christ, we receive the promise of a people and a land, except that by the time we reach Christ, the promise has grown even bigger. Paul says that Abraham received the promise that he would be heir of the world (Romans 4:13)! In Christ, we too are promised a home in the new creation.

Abraham wonders how this is all going to happen, as he is childless (Genesis 15:2). Instead of explaining or giving him a timetable, God says, 'Look up . . . count the stars – if indeed you can count them . . . So shall your offspring be' (verse 5). Now, in one sense, this is simply a reiteration of the promise. There's no new information there. But it's more than that, for God is saying, 'Don't just look at the problem. Don't just view things from your perspective. See the bigger picture! See my power spread across the skies! I have created a million, million burning suns, and I can create a million, million children to be my people.' And that's enough for Abraham. Abraham believed the promise because he trusted the promise-maker (verse 6).

Now God makes that promise to you. If you put your faith in Christ, then you can be part of God's new people, living in God's new world, a child of God and an heir of the world. Don't just look at your guilt and your shame. Don't just look at your fears and your doubts. Look up! Look up and see the power of God spread across the skies. See the million, million burning suns that God has made as a sign to us of his power to remake your life.

Look up! Look at the skies, the starry host. Look all around you at the evidence of God's faithfulness. Look back at how God kept his promise to Abraham by giving him a son, and the Israelites the Promised Land. Look at your own life and all that God has done – forgiving your sins and making you his child. Praise God; he is relentlessly faithful. Whatever fears, doubts or guilt threaten to overwhelm you, you can trust him for all that lies ahead today and for eternity.

Day 2

Read Genesis 15:1–21
Key verses: Genesis 15:8–10

· ·

8But Abram said, 'Sovereign LORD, how can I know that I shall gain possession of it?'

9So the LORD said to him, 'Bring me a heifer, a goat and a ram, each three years old, along with a dove and a young pigeon.'

10Abram brought all these to him, cut them in two and arranged the halves opposite each other; the birds, however, he did not cut in half.

Imagine a bride walking down the aisle to her groom.

They've said their vows, exchanged rings and signed the register. The couple not only make promises to each other, but they also enter into a legally binding 'till-death-do-us-part' contract.

Today, we make a contract by writing some commitments on a piece of paper and signing at the bottom.

In Abraham's day, you sliced up an animal and walked between the pieces. In effect, you were saying, 'If I break this covenant, may the fate of these animals be my fate!' So here, God is not only making a promise but also binding himself to that promise. Why? So that we can be doubly confident. A divine promise ought to be enough, because God never lies. There's a lovely little phrase in Isaiah 25:1 that literally says God is 'faithfully faithful'. We have a faithfully faithful God. But we get the bonus of having his promises signed and sealed in a covenant! 'How can I know?' asks Abraham in Genesis 15:8, and God's answer to that question is to call for the animals and to make a contract. This is how you can be sure, because it is signed and sealed in blood.

On the night before Jesus died, that contract was remade and reaffirmed. Here's Matthew's account of the Last Supper:

> Then [Jesus] took a cup, and when he had given thanks, he gave it to them, saying, 'Drink from it, all of you. This is my blood of the covenant, which is poured out for many for the forgiveness of sins.'
> (Matthew 26:27–28)

What did Jesus promise? He promised to forgive our sin. Whatever guilt you're carrying or whatever shame stains your soul, Christ promised to forgive you and, indeed, all who come to him. But he didn't just make a promise. He made a covenant – he bound himself to his promise. He signed and sealed it through bread and wine, and the following day, as he died on the cross, he delivered on that promise. He died in our place, that our sin might be forgiven. He shed his blood for us, and he remains true to that covenant to this day.

God is 'faithfully faithful' (see Isaiah 25:1). Meditate on this glorious truth. At the cross, we see God's covenant love and faithfulness in action. Jesus' broken body and shed blood are our guarantee that, no matter how heinous our sin or how frequently we have offended God, he will forgive us when we come to him. He knows how frail we are, how battered by sin. Today, accept God's invitation to bring your weary, burdened soul to him and receive afresh his promise of forgiveness.

Day 3

Read Genesis 15:1–21
Key verse: Genesis 15:1

....

After this, the word of the LORD came to Abram in a vision:

'Do not be afraid, Abram.
I am your shield,
your very great reward.'

It's not easy being a Christian. In fact, it can be really difficult. So is it really worth it?

What does Abraham get from this new covenant? First of all, he gains a son, Isaac. He also gets the people and the land that God had promised. But he receives much, much more. In chapter 14, Abraham has just restored to the king of Sodom what had been lost in battle. The king then tries to reward Abraham. It's really an invitation to come under his lordship. But Abraham refuses, saying to the king, 'You will never be able to say, "I made Abram rich"' (Genesis 14:23). Then chapter 15 begins: 'After this, the word of the LORD came to Abram in a vision . . . "I am your shield and your very great reward."' In other words, it's not the king of Sodom who will be Abraham's protector and benefactor; it is God himself. What is it that Abraham receives? Abraham gets God! His reward is God himself.

Abraham's response of faith is then credited to him as 'righteousness'. This means being right with God, being in a relationship with him as we were meant to be and made to be. It means that Abraham can come into God's presence, enjoy a relationship with God, enjoy God's love!

What did I get on my wedding day? I got about £100, a few dresses and some Jane Austen novels. When my wife said, 'All I have I thee endow', that's what was on offer. But I didn't marry her to get my hands on some books and dresses. What I got from our marriage covenant was my favourite person in the world. Think about these words from Martin Luther, the great Reformer:

> Faith unites us with Christ in the same way that a bride is united with her husband. Our sins, death and damnation, now belong to Christ, while his grace, life and salvation are now ours. For if Christ is a husband, he must take on himself those things which belonged to his bride, and he

must give to her, those things that are his. Not only that, he also gives us himself.

(Martin Luther, 'The Freedom of a Christian, 1520', *The Roots of Reform*, The Annotated Luther, Fortress Press, 2015, pp. 499–500)

I love that last line; it's beautiful. Luther lists some of the benefits that come to us in the Lord Jesus Christ. But best of all, we get Christ himself.

As the true God who always tells the truth, God cannot help but be faithful to his character, promises, purposes and glory. This faithfulness graciously and gloriously extends to us. In the midst of our suffering and struggles, God gives the very best he could give us; he gives us himself: 'I am your shield and very great reward.' He will never leave or betray you. He will love you for ever. You will always be welcome in his presence. You are his. Today, take joy in this incomparable treasure that is unreservedly yours.

Day 4

Read Genesis 15:1–21
Key verses: Genesis 15:17–18

....

> ¹⁷*When the sun had set and darkness had fallen, a smoking brazier with a blazing torch appeared and passed between the pieces.* ¹⁸*On that day the LORD made a covenant with Abram and said, 'To your descendants I give this land.'*

Can you picture the scene?

Laid out, on the ground, were the animals God had asked for. On one side: half a cow, half a goat and half a sheep, and a dove. There was no point cutting a dove in two, so it just goes off on one side. On the other side: the other half of the cow, the goat and the sheep, and a pigeon. The sun has set, darkness has fallen, then a 'smoking brazier' and a 'blazing torch' appear. They represent God. In fact, you might want to think of them almost as a kind of mini version of when God came down at Mount Sinai. So, God appears and passes through the animals, and it's in that key moment that the covenant is made (verse 17).

But what's missing from the picture? Abraham. He's not playing any part in the action. What is his role as this covenant is made? Absolutely none! 'As the sun was setting, Abram fell into a deep sleep, and a thick and dreadful darkness came over him' (verse 12). Abraham is asleep! He's out for the count. This is one of the key moments in the whole Bible story, in the whole of human history, and Abraham sleeps through it all.

To be fair to him, I don't think it was a normal sleep. It seems that it was a supernaturally induced sleep. The point is this: it's a one-way agreement. All the commitments are made by God. All the action is done by him. All Abraham does is receive: 'Abram believed the Lord, and he credited it to him as righteousness' (verse 6). His role is simply to receive the promises by faith. And when it comes to receiving Christ and his promises, here's what you have to do to be worthy – nothing. Absolutely nothing. There is nothing you need to do. No level of morality that you have to attain, no feat that you have to accomplish. No religious duty to perform, no kind of intellectual level of understanding that you have to attain – all you must do, and all you can do, is receive the promises by faith. This is what my sinful, doubting, fearful heart needs more than anything else: for God to reaffirm his covenant promises to me. We come because God promises to forgive, because God covenants to forgive.

Come to the cross. See God's love and faithfulness on display, his personal and passionate commitment to you. Just as he walked among the carcasses to pledge his faithfulness to Abraham, he went to the cross to bring you salvation. He did all that needed to be done – the penalty for sin has been done away with: 'It is finished' (John 19:30). Today, receive afresh this promise of forgiveness from a forever faithful God.

> Nothing in my hand I bring,
> Simply to Thy cross I cling;
> Naked, come to Thee for dress,
> Helpless, look to Thee for grace:
> Foul, I to the fountain fly,
> Wash me, Saviour, or I die.
> (Augustus Toplady, 'Rock of Ages', 1763)

1 Samuel

Israel had never had a king before. God had appointed judges to lead the people, but now a monarchy was to be established. 1 Samuel charts this transition to a new type of leadership under God. We don't know who wrote this book, but it is named after Samuel, the prophet and judge. He established the monarchy in Israel and anointed the first two kings: Saul and David.

As well as providing historical detail, 1 Samuel highlights what personal faithfulness to God looks like, as well as the reasons for, and consequences of, unfaithfulness.

Day 5

Read 1 Samuel 13:5–14
Key verses: 1 Samuel 13:11–12

....

¹¹ *'What have you done?' asked Samuel.*

Saul replied, 'When I saw that the men were scattering, and that you did not come at the set time, and that the Philistines were assembling at Michmash, ¹² *I thought, "Now the Philistines will come down against me at Gilgal, and I have not sought the* LORD*'s favour." So I felt compelled to offer the burnt offering.'*

What should we make of believers who start the Christian life with great promise but end in failure?

Saul had every reason to be a champion for God. He was born into privilege, had exceptional physical attributes and was God's anointed king. But this first moment of crisis in his leadership signalled the beginning of his decline. The Philistine army was arrayed against him. 'All the troops with him were quaking with fear. He waited for seven days, the time set by Samuel; but Samuel did not come to Gilgal, and Saul's men began to scatter' (verses 7–8).

Saul thought that he had to take action or the whole army would desert. So he sacrificed the burnt offerings himself (verse 9). Commentators struggle to define the actual sin of which Saul is guilty. But there is disobedience at the heart of it. ' "You have done a foolish thing," Samuel said. "You have not kept the command the LORD your God gave you" ' (verse 13). The consequences were severe – Saul's dynasty would end (verse 14) and his relationship with Samuel was irrevocably damaged (verse 15). What is happening here? By sacrificing, was Saul attempting to extend his powers to include a priestly role as well as a military one? Had he lost confidence in God? Was he failing to rely on God? We are given a clue when he says to Samuel, ' "I haven't even asked for the Lord's help!" So I felt compelled to offer the burnt offering myself' (verse 12, NLT). Saul didn't make time to listen to God, and had taken matters into his own hands.

We see a similar scenario in chapter 14. The Philistines were in disarray so Saul shouted to Ahijah, 'Bring the ephod here' (verse 18, NLT). The ephod (a garment worn by the high priest) was used to discern God's will, and Saul was expecting God to give him orders about how to handle this situation. But while he was talking to the priest, confusion among the Philistines increased and Saul said, 'Never mind; let's get going' (verse 19, NLT). Essentially, he was saying, 'We should be waiting for divine orders, but too much is happening. We haven't got time to wait for God.'

Saul's tragic failure begins as self-sufficiency grows in his heart. He has no time to wait for God, no time to listen.

Today, we come before almighty God – our all-knowing, ever-present, eternally powerful, sovereign God. With all the choices, responsibilities and conversations that lie ahead in our waking hours, we can't afford to say, 'Never mind; let's get going.' Make time to linger in God's presence, prayerfully admit your dependence on him and ask him to speak to you through his Word. Over the long haul, it is this daily decision, more than any other, that results in a life of faithfulness.

If we think we can do life on our own, we will not take prayer seriously.

(Paul E. Miller, *A Praying Life*, NavPress, 2009, p. 59)

Day 6

Read 1 Samuel 13:5–14
Key verse: 1 Samuel 13:13

....

'You have done a foolish thing,' Samuel said. 'You have not kept the command the LORD your God gave you; if you had, he would have established your kingdom over Israel for all time.'

Why didn't Saul just obey God?

Because Saul wasn't listening to God (see Day 5), his relationship with him had become distant, and so the confidence to trust and obey gradually eroded.

We see this pattern throughout Saul's reign. In 1 Samuel 15:2, God tells him, 'I have decided to settle accounts with the nation of Amalek' (NLT). The Amalekites had tried to prevent Israel from reaching Sinai after they had crossed through the Red Sea (see Exodus 17:14), so God was giving Saul the responsibility of carrying out the divine sentence. This wasn't a war of aggression or self-defence, but a truly holy war.

God decreed that the whole nation must be destroyed. This may seem harsh to us but it would not have seemed strange to the Israelites. They were carrying out God's judgment, and he would have the victory over the Amalekites. Saul engages in a great slaughter, but it was not the total destruction that the Lord had demanded. He spared Agag, the Amalekite king, and kept the best of the sheep and cattle (1 Samuel 15:7–9). What held Saul back from total obedience? We can't be sure, but no doubt it was similar to the things that hold us back. Perhaps saving the best of the livestock made him something of a hero in front of his men? It must have been to their advantage. Perhaps he hoped to negotiate a huge ransom for the release of King Agag?

In our materialistic, consumer-driven age, there is relentless pressure to hold back the best in our commitment to God. So often we have to choose between acceptance by our friends or total obedience to God. We rationalize our choices: 'To maintain this lifestyle for my family, I must achieve a certain income, which means I must work certain hours. I don't have any free time or money to give to God.' Although most of us could live comfortably with a much lesser lifestyle, we are reluctant to consider such a choice. Like Saul, we give God our leftovers rather than our best.

God held nothing back in his commitment to us – he gave his one and only Son to save us, and the Holy Spirit to live within us. Why would we hold back the best in our commitment to him?

Giving our best is not proved by one-off grand displays of devotion but, rather, in continuing obedience in the mundane and unremarkable routine of life. Part of this is faithfulness in giving from our finances.

> If you are truly submitted to the lordship of Christ, if you are willing to obey Him completely in every area of your life, your giving will reveal it. We will do many things before we will give someone else, even Christ, the rights over every dollar we have and ever will have. But if you have done that, it will be expressed in your giving. That's why it's said that your checkbook tells more about you than almost anything else.
> (Donald S. Whitney, *Spiritual Disciplines for the Christian Life*, NavPress, 2014, p. 177)

Day 7

Read 1 Samuel 13:5–14
Key verses: 1 Samuel 13:13–14

....

> ¹³ *'You have done a foolish thing,' Samuel said. 'You have not kept the command the Lord your God gave you; if you had, he would have established your kingdom over Israel for all time. ¹⁴ But now your kingdom will not endure; the Lord has sought out a man after his own heart and appointed him ruler of his people, because you have not kept the Lord's command.'*

Is there a way back to God after failure?

Yes. But only if we repent. Unfortunately, Saul never learned how to do this. Instead, he justified his disobedient actions. He excused burning the offerings because his men were scattering and Samuel had not arrived at the appointed time (verse 11). In 1 Samuel 15, when Saul finally admitted that he'd disobeyed the Lord's commands, he was quick to justify himself and explain the mitigating circumstances: 'I was afraid of the people and did what they demanded' (verse 24, NLT).

Compare Saul's repentance to King David's. The moment Nathan the prophet exposed David's sins of committing adultery with Bathsheba and murdering her husband Uriah, David repented without any attempt at self-justification (2 Samuel 12). In Psalm 51:3–4, he confesses to God:

> For I know my transgressions,
>> and my sin is always before me.
> Against you, you only, have I sinned
>> and done what is evil in your sight;
> so you are right in your verdict
>> and justified when you judge.

As well as attempting to justify himself, Saul also tries to spiritualize his failures. In 1 Samuel 15:15, he says the army spared the best of the cattle and sheep to sacrifice them to God, so that, ultimately, God's command of total destruction would be fulfilled. Samuel, in verse 22, replies:

> Does the LORD delight in burnt offerings and sacrifices
>> as much as in obeying the LORD?
> To obey is better than sacrifice,
>> and to heed is better than the fat of rams.

Like Saul, we may attend public worship but God wants our faithfulness to be more than skin-deep. He is longing for our wholehearted devotion. If you have not been obeying God, turn back in repentance today. None of us has to finish like Saul. The example of David assures us of that. He fell spectacularly and, in some ways, his fall was greater than Saul's. But his repentance and determination to live once again in faithful obedience to God were equally spectacular and truly moving.

God's faithfulness to us is expressed, in part, in his readiness to forgive: 'If we confess our sins, he is faithful and just and will forgive us our sins and purify us from all unrighteousness' (1 John 1:9).

If you want to get back on the road of faithful obedience, follow the instructions Jesus gave to the Ephesian church in Revelation 2:5:

- *'Consider how far you have fallen!'* Think back to the days when you loved Jesus more. Reflect how and why your relationship with Jesus has changed.
- *'Repent.'* Turn back to God in sorrow. Find joy in his mercy and willingness to help you renew your commitment to him.

- *'Do the things you did at first.'* When you were walking closer with God, no doubt you had a hunger for his Word, spent time in his presence, told others about him and loved being with your church family. Start doing these things again and begin to enjoy an intimate relationship with the Father who is waiting to restore you.

Psalms

The book of Psalms is the collection of prayers and songs used by the Israelites for their personal and corporate worship. Written by a variety of authors, including King David, each psalm is carefully crafted poetry, rich in imagery. Although written for specific contexts, the psalms teach us how to worship, confess our sin and cry out to God. They portray God as King, Creator, Judge, Redeemer, Helper and Deliverer. The psalms teach us about God's faithfulness and give us words – amid our fears, doubts and questions – to declare our love for him and our desire to be faithful.

Day 8

Read Psalm 119:97–104
Key verses: Psalm 119:101–102

....

> [101]*I have kept my feet from every evil path*
>   *so that I might obey your word.*
> [102]*I have not departed from your laws,*
>   *for you yourself have taught me.*

Imagine that you're on a plane and the pilot announces, 'Good morning, ladies and gentlemen. As you know, we are committed to your safety. I want you to know that I don't plan on crashing very much.' How about not crashing at all? The objective must be 'I don't plan on crashing at all!'

Are we as clear about our objectives when it comes to sinning? The psalmist is uncompromising. We are to keep our feet from '*every* evil path' so that we can obey God's Word.

This principle is not just a moralistic one. Rather, it is written in the same tone as Paul's words to the Colossians:

'Now, let's become what we are in Christ. You are united to Christ. Therefore, seek those things from above where Christ is seated. Your life is hidden with Christ in God. This is who you are, your identity, and God has given you his Word to help you to become who and what he has designed you to be' (a paraphrase of Colossians 3:1–10).

Psalm 119:102 reminds us that we will never stop sinning because someone else persuaded us to do so; it will take the Word of God, by the Spirit of God: 'You yourself have taught me.' But there is no contradiction between the declarations in verses 101 and 102. We are both, at the same time, entirely dependent on the work of the Holy Spirit and yet entirely responsible for keeping our feet from 'every evil path'.

God has never yet turned a television programme off for me! The Lord has never taken a book right out of my hands! But I have heard the Spirit of God say, 'I thought you were reading Psalm 119, where it says keep yourself from "every evil path". And have you read Philippians 4, where it says, "Whatever is pure, whatever is lovely, whatever is admirable, think about these things"?'

The reason why you and I have not deviated from our course and lost connection with the source of God's grace is not because of superior virtue or peculiar discernment.

It is because we have not departed from God's laws, for he himself has taught us (Psalm 119:102). We have to make sure we are listening to, meditating on and applying God's Word to our lives because it is the source of wisdom and the means of faithfulness.

This theme is consistent throughout the Bible. John says, 'See that what you have heard from the beginning remains in you. If it does, you also will remain in the Son and in the Father' (1 John 2:24). Similarly, Paul says to Timothy, 'Continue in what you have learned and have become convinced of, because you know those from whom you learned it, and how from infancy you have known the Holy Scriptures, which are able to make you wise for salvation' (2 Timothy 3:14–15).

Meditate on Psalm 119:101–102.

- Thank God for the ways in which he has kept you from evil, by teaching you through his Word and by the power of the Holy Spirit.
- Ask for God's help to be uncompromising as you tackle sin in your life.
- Pray that you would continue to obey God's Word, so that you remain faithful to him.

Acts

Acts was the second volume written by Doctor Luke. His first, his Gospel, sets out what Jesus 'began to do and to teach' (Acts 1:1), and this book explains what Jesus continued to do through the apostles' preaching and the growth of the church. Acts is a selective account of the first thirty years of the church's life. It describes the relentless progress of the gospel from Jerusalem to Rome, the lives and ministry of Peter and Paul, and the role of the Holy Spirit.

The book of Acts shows believers being faithful to Jesus' commission to be his witnesses (Acts 1:8). Their obedience meant being faithful to the message and spread of the gospel, regardless of suffering, and faithful to God's vision for the church.

Day 9

Read Acts 20:17–38
Key verses: Acts 20:17–19

....

¹⁷ *From Miletus, Paul sent to Ephesus for the elders of the church.* ¹⁸*When they arrived, he said to them: 'You know how I lived the whole time I was with you, from the first day I came into the province of Asia.* ¹⁹*I served the Lord with great humility and with tears and in the midst of severe testing by the plots of my Jewish opponents.'*

Does what you do match what you say? Does your walk match your talk?

For Paul, it certainly did (verses 18 and 33–35). He was able to appeal to the Ephesian elders as witnesses of the way in which his life matched his words. Such integrity was the essential ingredient for proclaiming a credible gospel message (verse 24) and also for making mature disciples.

This faithful conduct allowed Paul to remind the Thessalonians of how he and his fellow workers *lived*. The 'gospel came to you not simply with words but also with power, with the Holy Spirit and deep conviction. You know how we lived among you for your sake' (1 Thessalonians 1:5). The gospel that Paul was proclaiming was bearing fruit in his own life, and it was this combination of word and life that made his gospel communication so effective.

That is why he urges the Ephesian elders to 'keep watch over' themselves (Acts 20:28). He pleads with them to take their spiritual condition seriously. It is only when the leaders themselves remain faithful to God in their discipleship that they can expect others to be so too. It is only as they grow in grace and in the knowledge of the Lord Jesus, pressing on in the faith, that they can appeal to others to do so. Neglect in this area leaves us spiritually dry, often drifting morally, prone to mere professionalism, and passing on information without any real connection to our own spiritual life and maturity. Paul's words to Timothy should ring in our ears:

> Set an example for the believers in speech, in conduct, in love, in faith and in purity . . . Watch your life and doctrine closely. Persevere in them, because if you do, you will save both yourself and your hearers.
> (1 Timothy 4:12, 16)

There was nothing in Paul's life that could be used as an excuse by other people for not believing the gospel. His message was wedded to a godly life that made his ministry credible. In just the same way, our lives must embody the truth of the gospel. Faithful gospel proclamation and consistent living must go hand in hand in whatever area of mission or ministry God calls us to – the combination is vital.

Always living with integrity – so that what you say about the gospel truly resonates with how you live your life – is a huge responsibility. You can't do it on your own, but you don't need to. God, in his faithfulness, gives us his grace to live faithfully!

> Now this is our boast: our conscience testifies that we have conducted ourselves in the world, and especially in our relations with you, with integrity and godly sincerity. We have done so, relying not on worldly wisdom but on God's grace.
> (2 Corinthians 1:12)

Today, rely on God's grace to put his truth on display in your life faithfully.

Day 10

Read Acts 20:17–38

Key verses: Acts 20:22–24

. . . .

22'And now, compelled by the Spirit, I am going to Jerusalem, not knowing what will happen to me there. 23I only know that in every city the Holy Spirit warns me that prison and hardships are facing me. 24However, I consider my life worth nothing to me; my only aim is to finish the race and complete the task the Lord Jesus has given me – the task of testifying to the good news of God's grace.'

'I have fought the good fight, I have finished the race, I have kept the faith' (2 Timothy 4:7). Paul's words to Timothy sum up his faithfulness to God and to all that God had called him to do. But this faithfulness was costly.

In Acts 20:3, Luke refers to the plots of the Jews against Paul. In verse 19, Paul says, 'I served the Lord with great humility and with tears and in the midst of severe testing by the plots of my Jewish opponents.' Like the Lord Jesus who called him, if obedience required it, Paul was willing to suffer, which is the only way that you can make sense of the two apparently contradictory messages of the Spirit in verses 22 and 23. Verse 22 describes how the Spirit compels Paul to go to Jerusalem, yet in the very next verse the same Spirit warns Paul that he will suffer if he does go. How can such an apparent contradiction be reconciled? Only by Paul's statement of purpose in verse 24: 'However, I consider my life worth nothing to me; my only aim is to finish the race and complete the task the Lord Jesus has given me – the task of testifying to the good news of God's grace.' Paul was willing to suffer – to give everything he had – to make disciples, precisely because he knew that God had called him and given him an urgent task to fulfil.

Paul's motivation was absolutely clear. He knew the purpose of his life and calling, and he was willing to lay down his life if necessary. He wasn't after fame or money. His ambition was not to climb an ecclesiastical ladder but to finish the race, to complete the task of proclaiming the gospel and making disciples.

Similarly, our calling to serve God today, with its privilege of bringing the good news to others, should not be driven by self-fulfilment but by the calling of Jesus Christ himself. Acts 20 shows us that there are no false promises, no immediate rewards, save knowing that we serve Christ faithfully as we fulfil the task he has given us.

'Go and make disciples' (Matthew 28:19) was Jesus' charge to his disciples and, in turn, to the church. For pastors and ministry leaders, the mandate is clear (although the outworking may be more of a challenge!). But each of us, with our own unique set of circumstances and relationships, can be disciple-makers as we invest spiritually in children, grandchildren, those in our home groups or the young person interning in our church. Investing in others for the long haul is costly but part of our calling as disciples. Today, pray for God's help to be faithful in the task of pointing others to the Lord Jesus.

1 Thessalonians and 2 Timothy

1 Thessalonians

The first epistle to the Thessalonians is essentially a follow-up letter to new Christians. Persecution had forced Paul and his companions to flee the busy seaport city of Thessalonica sooner than he would have wished, leaving behind a group of very new Jewish and Gentile converts (Acts 17:1–10). Paul wrote to these believers from Corinth to encourage them to stand firm in the face of persecution. The letter also provides instruction about the second coming of Christ that Paul had hoped to give in person. He prays for these believers, who had started off so well, to be faithful and to continue making spiritual progress.

2 Timothy

This letter records Paul's last words. He was in prison, chained to a Roman soldier, dictating this letter to Luke for his young pastor friend, Timothy, Paul's 'true son in the faith' (1 Timothy 1:2). Timothy had been his travelling companion on missionary journeys, had visited churches on his behalf, was with him during his first stint in prison and was now the pastor of the church in Ephesus. Paul wrote to Timothy, encouraging him to visit but, more importantly, pleading with him to stay faithful, keeping Christ and the gospel central to his life and ministry.

Day 11

Read 1 Thessalonians 2:1–12
Key verses: 1 Thessalonians 2:1–2

....

¹*You know, brothers and sisters, that our visit to you was not without results.* ²*We had previously suffered and been treated outrageously in Philippi, as you know, but with the help of our God we dared to tell you his gospel in the face of strong opposition.*

How can we effectively engage with our culture while, at the same time, staying faithful to the gospel message?

Paul's secret was that while he contextualized the gospel, he never relativized it. To relativize the gospel is to wrap it up and put it in the culture. To contextualize the gospel is to understand it and make sure it connects with the culture without changing the message.

A great example of contextualization is Paul's engagement with those seeking the 'unknown god' at Mars Hill (Acts 17:16–34). He didn't start the conversation by telling

the people of Athens all the ways in which they were wrong in their understanding. Instead, he said, 'I see you have an altar here; you are seeking the truth. Let me begin with where you are and take you on a journey, so that you can see the truth for what it really is.'

The fundamental challenge for us today is whether we believe the Scriptures speak the true Word of God and therefore have the power to transform culture. Alternatively, do we believe culture should transform our understanding of what the Bible teaches?

Our job is not to fit into the culture or change our core message to be popular. As Christians, we often think society should welcome and embrace us. Instead, the New Testament tells us that we will be challenged, mocked and persecuted (John 16:33). Paul says, 'With the help of our God we dared to tell you his gospel in the face of strong opposition' (1 Thessalonians 2:2). Acts 16 records Paul's being thrown into prison in Philippi because of his faithfulness to the gospel. Wherever he went, there was either a revival or a riot!

Will you dare to be faithful to God – at work, as a local church or in your family – in the face of strong opposition? Will you live out what you believe, not expecting the culture to embrace you but recognizing that it

probably won't? We have a choice: we can be faithful to what God has called us to be and do, or we can be absorbed into our culture, quickly losing our effectiveness as the body of Christ and our witness in the world.

Heavenly Father, thank you that the Lord Jesus was faithful to you and to me – enduring the mocking, the betrayal, the nails and then dying in my place. He is not just an example to follow but is praying for me and is with me, by the power of the Holy Spirit, enabling me to be faithful.

Today, I pray for myself and my church community. Help us to stay faithful to you in the face of opposition, whether we are being mocked for our faith by family members, challenged at work because of our beliefs or feeling the sting of increasing marginalization in society. Help us to stay faithful to the gospel, in the way we present it to others and the way in which we live our lives. May our conversations be marked with love, kindness and wisdom, so that the only offence is that of the cross. For Jesus' glory we pray. Amen.

Day 12

Read 1 Thessalonians 2:1–12
Key verses: 1 Thessalonians 2:2 and 4

....

²With the help of our God we dared to tell you his gospel in the face of strong opposition . . . ⁴we speak as those approved by God to be entrusted with the gospel. We are not trying to please people but God, who tests our hearts.

What is the gospel?

Paul says, 'With the help of our God we dared to tell you *his* gospel' (verse 2, emphasis added). You could translate it 'the gospel of God', which Paul does in verses 8 and 9. In verse 4, he talks about being entrusted with the gospel and, in verse 13, he speaks twice about the power of the Word of God. For the apostle, there is the conviction that the gospel cannot be changed; it is something he is entrusted with.

We think that the gospel is ours, in the sense that we own it, or we redefine it to make it sound as if God calls us just to be nice people – but that is not the gospel! We don't have to guess the gospel message or try to work it out. Paul tells us exactly what it is:

> For what I received I passed on to you as of first importance: that Christ died for our sins according to the Scriptures, that he was buried, that he was raised on the third day according to the Scriptures, and that he appeared to Cephas, and then to the Twelve.
> (1 Corinthians 15:3–5)

The good news of the gospel is that Christ died in our place, paying the penalty our sins deserved. All we must do – all we can do – to be reconciled to God is to repent of our sins and trust in Christ's work on the cross. He not only died for us; his resurrection is the guarantee that one day we too will rise to new life and spend eternity with God. No wonder Paul could say with confidence: 'I am not ashamed of the gospel, because it is the power of God that brings salvation to everyone who believes' (Romans 1:16). Paul's radical faithfulness was built on these truths and his conviction that the gospel worked.

Our faithfulness hinges on the same things. We are not free to change the gospel. It is a baton that has been handed to us, one that we must pass on to the generation that comes after us. We can't dilute it or turn it into something else because this is the only message that has the power to break the power of sin, transform lives and conquer death. We are not called to be nice people or just to make a difference. We are called to make disciples and point people to this glorious good news.

Have you ever found yourself wanting to soften the edges of the gospel when sharing it with someone? Have you wanted to lessen the demand for repentance, the brutality of the cross or the wrath of God? While we don't have to convey all the elements of the gospel in every conversation, we do need to make sure it is God's gospel we're sharing, otherwise we have nothing to offer people. And this message of good news is not just for unbelievers! Meditate on 1 Corinthians 15:3–5; speak it to your own soul and hold fast to this gospel, which proclaims freedom from sin and death, forgiveness and eternal security, and the power of God at work in you today.

Day 13

Read 1 Thessalonians 2:1–12
Key verses: 1 Thessalonians 2:3–7

••

> ³*For the appeal we make does not spring from error or impure motives, nor are we trying to trick you.* ⁴*On the contrary, we speak as those approved by God to be entrusted with the gospel. We are not trying to please people but God, who tests our hearts.* ⁵*You know we never used flattery, nor did we put on a mask to cover up greed – God is our witness.* ⁶*We were not looking for praise from people, not from you or anyone else, even though as apostles of Christ we could have asserted our authority.* ⁷*Instead, we were like young children among you.*

What was at the heart of Paul's life that made him so faithful to God?

Essentially, Paul understood that God had commissioned him to proclaim the gospel message, and his life was now about pleasing him. So, Paul refused to dabble in error, or with impure motives or misunderstanding. He didn't want to make money; he wasn't interested in persuading people unfairly; he wasn't going to tell them a lie; and he wasn't going to water down the message. His actions weren't driven by the strength of his personality and he wasn't swayed by what people thought of him.

We may not share Paul's particular commission, but we are called by God to live for God alone. So, don't allow yourself to lower the standard of the gospel just to be popular. Don't turn the gospel into something you make money out of. Don't turn the church into a glorified social club. Instead, have confidence in the fact that when God calls, he equips and enables us to live for him.

Paul's confidence in God's calling meant that he acted with integrity and faithfulness, regardless of the circumstances or occasion. We have a glimpse of what this looked like in the 'holy' and 'blameless' (verse 10) way he lived among the Thessalonians – comforting, encouraging and urging them to continue in the faith. He explains that he didn't try to manipulate them: 'Instead, we were like young children among you' (verse 7). This is a picture of innocence and trust. Then he switches to three other pictures.

He says that he was like a nursing mother caring for them. His language is tender, gentle and kind. Next, he addresses them as brothers and sisters, bringing an equality into his relationship with them. He also uses the image of a father, as he challenges, guides and helps believers to understand how they are to live for God in the world in which they find themselves.

Your faithfulness matters! Your children, parents, spouse, friends and work colleagues are watching your life. They notice how you cope with suffering, how you treat others, your attitude to money, your integrity, your commitment to church and your passion for the gospel. Your example to others is never neutral – it is either positive or negative. If, like Paul, you live for an audience of One, you will spur others on in their faith. Put your name in the following verse and pray for God's help to live a life worth imitating.

Remember _____, who spoke the word of God to you. Consider the outcome of their way of life and imitate their faith.

(Hebrews 13:7)

Day 14

Read 1 Thessalonians 5:1–28

Key verses: 1 Thessalonians 5:6–8

....

6So then, let us not be like others, who are asleep, but let us be awake and sober. 7For those who sleep, sleep at night, and those who get drunk, get drunk at night. 8But since we belong to the day, let us be sober, putting on faith and love as a breastplate, and the hope of salvation as a helmet.

Are you an early bird or a night owl?

In Paul's terms, believers are all daytime people. We are to be clear-headed and alert, not morally and spiritually asleep, so that we can live for the day when Jesus returns. The verb translated 'sleep' in these verses refers to moral laxity, not death (see Mark 13:36). We are no longer in spiritual darkness by circumstance or by nature (Colossians 1:13, 21–22). We have a new position, nature and loyalty (Galatians 2:20). Consequently, we have a responsibility to be morally alert and to have a distinctive way of life (Ephesians 5:8–15).

Paul likens our new lifestyle to warfare and urges us to 'Put on the full armour of God, so that you can take your stand against the devil's schemes' (Ephesians 6:11). We are to wear the armour that is our characteristic hallmark as believers – faith, hope and love.

This is the third time Paul has reminded the Thessalonian believers about this trio. In 1 Thessalonians 1:3, he looked back and acknowledged the genuineness of their salvation because he saw their faith, hope and love. In verses 6–10, Paul was delighted because the believers had resisted temptation. What was the victory? They were standing firm in the Lord. They were people of endurance, going on with the Christian basics of faith and love.

For us, the return of Christ requires nothing dramatic by way of preparation. We are just to go on – with faith, hope and love – trusting God, come what may, and living in the obedience of faith. We must go on loving our fellow believers and reaching out beyond them in love to the world. And we go on with endurance and hope, as we keep our eyes fixed on the Lord Jesus who is returning. That's our armour. We put on the breastplate of faith and love, and the hope of salvation as our helmet, so that we are protected, equipped and ready to live for the day of Christ's return.

God is 'abounding in love and faithfulness' (Exodus 34:6): he has redeemed us (Colossians 1:14) and reconciled us to himself (Colossians 1:22), and he will return (Acts 1:10–11; Revelation 22:20). He now 'lives' in us (Galatians 2:20) and gives us the resources to be faithful to him (2 Peter 1:3).

What does God want in return? Not an extravagant display of devotion – he has already provided that – but moment-by-moment faithfulness. This requires daily putting our armour on:

God is strong, and he wants you strong. So take everything the Master has set out for you, well-made weapons of the best materials. And put them to use so you will be able to stand up to everything the Devil throws your way. This is no afternoon athletic contest that we'll walk away from and forget about in a couple of hours. This is for keeps, a life-or-death fight to the finish against the Devil and all his angels.

(Ephesians 6:10–12, MSG)

Day 15

Read 1 Thessalonians 5:1–28
Key verses: 1 Thessalonians 5:9–11

· ·

⁹For God did not appoint us to suffer wrath but to receive salvation through our Lord Jesus Christ. ¹⁰He died for us so that, whether we are awake or asleep, we may live together with him. ¹¹Therefore encourage one another and build each other up, just as in fact you are doing.

Imagine if, on the day when Jesus chooses to return, we are having a spiritual 'day off', that we are not living for the Lord Jesus as we should be doing. We are dozing spiritually. And our lives are showing some evidence of moral and spiritual slackness. Imagine that the day before Jesus' return is a Sunday, when we are passionately 'on fire' for God. The next day, Monday, when he comes back, we are below par, spiritually speaking. What will happen to us when the Lord returns?

Paul deals with this very issue in verse 10. 'Asleep' is not the verb that means we are dead and living with Jesus; it indicates the possibility of moral and spiritual slackness. And 'awake' means what it has meant in previous verses: being alert for the coming Lord. The apostle offers us the most intense, remarkable and glorious comfort. He says our great confidence in relation to Christ's coming is not anything that we do or are, but what God in Christ has done for us. We have been appointed eternally for the personal and full possession of salvation, through our Lord Jesus Christ who 'died for us' (verse 10).

His death covers all our sins, including those sins of spiritual slackness. Of course, we are to spur one another on to live in faith, love and hope (see Day 14), and some of what that looks like is described in 1 Thessalonians 5:12–22. But we can look forward to the second coming of Christ with confidence because the One who returns is that perfect mediator who knows both God's requirements and our needs. By his knowledge, this 'righteous servant' has justified many (Isaiah 53:11). We stand before Christ, clothed in his righteousness alone.

Your eternal destiny is not dependent on whether you are having a good or a bad day, spiritually speaking, when Jesus returns. In fact, it is not dependent on what *you do* at all. It is solely dependent on what *Jesus has done* on the cross. His faithfulness guarantees the security of our salvation:

> He was pierced for our transgressions,
>   he was crushed for our iniquities;
> the punishment that brought us peace was on him,
>   and by his wounds we are healed.
> (Isaiah 53:5)

Let this truth amaze, humble and comfort you. And as you meet others today who are also conscious of their wandering hearts and disappointed by the coolness of their affection for Christ, let the reminder of Christ's faithfulness encourage you and build you up (verse 11). Allow it to spur you on in your devotion to him.

Day 16

Read 1 Thessalonians 5:1–28
Key verses: 1 Thessalonians 5:23–24

....

²³May God himself, the God of peace, sanctify you through and through. May your whole spirit, soul and body be kept blameless at the coming of our Lord Jesus Christ. ²⁴The one who calls you is faithful, and he will do it.

'I'll never be ready for when Jesus comes!'

Paul issues a whole raft of different commands – some with expansions and additions (verses 15–22). There are commands about how we are to treat leaders, and others about our personal obligations. All of these are about how we are to live in readiness for Christ's return. They describe the lifestyle required of a church family, and believers are to behave this way to everybody, all the time. Some commands relate to our character – we are to be patient, non-retaliatory and good (verses 14–15); others relate to our spirituality and how to live before

God – we ought to be rejoicing, praying and giving thanks (verses 16–18).

The bar is high. The range of commands seems overwhelming. How can we be faithful to all God's requirements and so be ready for Jesus' second coming?

Paul concludes his letter by reminding the Thessalonians, and us, of a vital truth: we have God himself on our side. Verse 23 means that the heavenly Father will see to it that no single blemish will spoil the day of his Son's return. As Paul says in Philippians 1:6, 'He who began a good work in you will carry it on to completion until the day of Christ Jesus.' God will go on putting the finishing touches to the work he has begun in our lives and, when the day of Christ comes, everything will be ready for his return.

God himself promises that he will sanctify you. God will preserve you, in an all-embracing, completed holiness that touches every part of your being and covers all that you are. That's what the two words 'sanctify' and 'keep' mean in verse 23. He will preserve you in relation to himself (your 'spirit'); he will preserve you in relation to your personality (your 'soul'); and he will preserve you in holy living in your body. We can have every confidence in God's promise to do this because he is the faithful and sufficient God: 'The one who calls you is faithful, and he will do it' (verse 24). Praise God!

Is our faithfulness important if, ultimately, it all depends on God's faithfulness? Yes! How we live as Christians matters. The genuineness of our salvation is proved by a new desire to obey God. Our spiritual transformation to become more like Jesus testifies to God's power at work in us, changing our hearts, minds and wills. God grants us the privilege of being his 'fellow workers' (2 Corinthians 6:1).

But – thank God – at every point our fragile and often wavering faithfulness is enabled, undergirded and completed by the faithfulness of Christ. Today, meditate, rest and rejoice in the truth that 'The one who calls you is faithful, and he will do it' (verse 24).

Day 17

Read 2 Timothy 4:1–22
Key verses: 2 Timothy 4:6–7

....

⁶For I am already being poured out like a drink offering, and the time for my departure is near. ⁷I have fought the good fight, I have finished the race, I have kept the faith.

How do we make sure that we finish life well?

Paul is a great example for us. In this poignant farewell chapter, he describes himself as a sacrifice, 'a drink offering' poured out before his Lord (verse 6). He knows that he is about to die: 'The time of my departure is near.' The Greek word for departure conveys the idea of being set free. It is the word used when a boat leaves harbour. For Paul, it is not a reluctant departure but a purposeful one. He is packed, ready to go and looking forward to all that lies ahead.

He uses three pictures derived from 2 Timothy 2 to describe his faithfulness: the retiring soldier – 'I have fought the good fight'; the retiring athlete – 'I have finished the race'; the retiring farmer – 'I have kept the faith', which means literally 'I have persevered', like a farmer who has fulfilled his tasks. Jesus ran the race before him, enduring the cross and despising the shame (Hebrews 12:2). Now Paul is writing in chains but looking at the joy set before him, the 'Well done!' garland given to God's servant by the righteous judge.

Paul's example and his teaching encourage Timothy – and us – to run the race in the same way. People will come and go. There will be those, such as Demas, who love this present world (2 Timothy 4:10). There will be people like faithful Luke, practical Mark and evil Alexander (verses 11 and 14). There will be practical needs, such as for clothing and books, and there will be periods of living simply and tough times (verses 13 and 16–17). There will be love and encouragement from various Christian families, and there will be those, such as Trophimus, who will fall ill and won't be healed (verses 19–20). In the midst of it all, we must commit ourselves to the Lord and keep the gospel central. As individuals, we must come to God for daily cleansing and equipping. As a body of believers, we must spur one another on and invest in training, so that each and every man and woman in the church, by God's grace and mercy, might be able to say at the end of their lives, 'I have fought the good fight, I have finished the race, I have kept the faith.'

Paul's final word to Timothy and to the church was: 'The Lord be with your spirit. Grace be with you all' (verse 22). In this race of life, we can press on and finish well, knowing that God is with us personally and his grace is with us all for ever.

The Greeks had a race in their Olympic games that was unique. The winner was not the runner who finished first. It was the runner who finished with his torch still lit. I want to run all the way with the flame of my torch still lit for Him.

(Joseph M. Stowell, *Fan the Flame*, Moody Press, 1986, p. 32)

Day 18

Read 2 Timothy 4:1–22

Key verses: 2 Timothy 4:9–10

∙∙∙

⁹Do your best to come to me quickly, ¹⁰for Demas, because he loved this world, has deserted me and has gone to Thessalonica.

Last words are important.

These verses in 2 Timothy 4 are among the last known words of the apostle Paul. He is in prison in Rome, facing certain death. But as he writes his own epitaph – he has fought the fight, kept the faith, run the race and finished the course – he also pens one for another dear friend, Demas: 'Demas . . . has deserted me.'

Paul is not writing as a megalomaniac growing old in his loneliness but as the pastor of this man's soul. These two verses summarize nearly all that we know about Demas (he is mentioned in passing in Colossians 4:14 and Philemon 1:24 as a fellow worker with Luke and John

Mark). He serves as a warning of the grave possibility of spiritual decline in professing servants of God.

- *Demas deserted his divine call.* 'Demas has left me in the lurch' might serve as a translation of verse 10. Demas had abandoned Paul in his hour of greatest need. When Paul made his pleas before Caesar, no one stood with him. Unlike the other men Paul mentions in this chapter, Demas hadn't left him to take the gospel message elsewhere. Rather, he had deserted Christ's cause. Perhaps Thessalonica (where he had gone) was Demas' home town, the place where he was brought to Christ (Acts 17). In the mighty work of God there, perhaps Demas was one of those who had 'turned to God from idols to serve the living and true God' (1 Thessalonians 1:9). When he joined Paul, no doubt there were high hopes for him in Christian ministry. But this sense of destiny came to nothing because he deserted his divine calling.

- *Demas deserted the apostle Paul.* Demas had been in a privileged position. He'd seen Paul's suffering and the Lord standing by him; he had heard Paul preaching and witnessed him applying God's Word; he had seen answers to prayer, the glory of God and the power of the Holy Spirit coming down on men and women. And he had been drawn into intimate companionship with this great servant of God. But still he had deserted him.

- *Demas deserted the place of sacrifice and suffering.* He left Paul in Rome to face the judgment of Caesar. Demas would not face the tribulation, persecution and cost of following Christ. He was like the rocky soil in Jesus' parable of the sower (Matthew 13:1–23). There the Word of God is received with gladness but then, when the noon-day sun of trials and persecution begins to emerge, the Word fails to flourish in the life of the believer; it withers and fades and seems to die. We never find out whether Demas returned to Christ or had committed the final apostasy.

It is one thing to begin enthusiastically; it is another to continue.

Be sure to fear the Lord and serve him faithfully with all your heart; consider what great things he has done for you.
(1 Samuel 12:24)

Meditate on the 'great things [God] has done for you'.

- Pray that God's faithfulness would spur you on to 'serve him faithfully'.

- Pray for family members and friends who professed to be Christians but have wandered away from the faith. Ask God to bring these prodigals home.
- Pray for your pastor, elders, small group leaders and young people involved in ministry to stay faithful to God, to finish the Christian race well.

Day 19

Read 2 Timothy 4:1–22
Key verses: 2 Timothy 4:9–10

• •

⁹Do your best to come to me quickly, ¹⁰for Demas, because he loved this world, has deserted me and has gone to Thessalonica.

Have you ever noticed how quickly the opportunity to sin arises once you have decided to give in to temptation?

Demas fled to Thessalonica. Perhaps he was returning to his home town (see Day 18). It may have been that Thessalonica, rather than Rome, was the place God seemed to be blessing, and so was a much cosier place in which he could serve Christ. Yet it is striking that not only did Demas head to Thessalonica but also, in those difficult circumstances, that he was able to get there at all. How often, in the life of a professing child of God, the desire to flee the place of God's calling and appointment is almost invariably followed by the opportunity to do so.

There is a catalogue of names in Scripture that bear witness to this undying tactic of Satan.

Remember David. It was the time when kings go to war. But he ignored his place of duty, at the head of the army (2 Samuel 11:1). Soon afterwards, he committed adultery with Bathsheba and had her husband Uriah murdered. It all started because he saw the woman from his rooftop when he should have been at war.

Think of Jonah. He was fleeing from the Word of God and looking for an opportunity to escape it. He went to the port of Joppa and found a ship bound for Tarshish (Jonah 1:1–3).

Simon Peter wanted to flee from the cost of serving Christ, and then a servant-girl asked him if he had been with Jesus (Matthew 26:31–35, 57–58, 69–75). Demas-like, out of his heart and mouth, came the denial of the Lord Jesus.

It is true, in a very profound sense, that in the spiritual life you get what you want. When the desire to sin – to flee from God, his Word and his will – arises, the opportunity to do so will soon follow. Paul's highlighting that Demas 'loved this world' may imply that he turned away entirely from following Jesus. If so, Demas illustrates to us that when someone desires to turn away, he or she has no security with which to strengthen the soul against the onslaught of the devil. The immediate consequence of this spiritual decline was the opportunity to flee from Christ.

What do you really want? In spiritual terms, what are you aiming for?

There is a Cherokee tale about a man teaching his grandson about the war that wages in our souls. He explained that there are two wolves battling inside each one of us. One is evil – he is anger, envy, greed and resentment. The other wolf is good – he is joy, peace, hope and love. The young boy thought for a moment and then asked, 'Which wolf wins?' The old man replied simply, 'The one you feed.'

If we want to be like Christ, instead of fleeing *from* God as soon as temptation strikes, we need to flee *to* him – feeding on his Word and finding nourishment for our souls in prayer, worship, fellowship and service. Today, sinful desires *will* wage war within you, but don't feed them. Rather, keep your goal of Christlikeness in mind as you flee to him, finding strength for your soul.

Day 20

Read 2 Timothy 4:1–22
Key verses: 2 Timothy 4:9–10

....

⁹*Do your best to come to me quickly,* ¹⁰*for Demas, because he loved this world, has deserted me and has gone to Thessalonica.*

What causes backsliding?

Paul's answer in this case is that 'Demas loved this world'. The apostle is not speaking of the world around us, the cosmos in all its beauty and glory. He is thinking of the age in which we live, which is given over to the powers of evil and darkness. In Galatians 1:4, Paul calls it 'the present evil age'. It may be better to translate verse 10 as 'Demas has forsaken me because he fell in love with this age'.

Like Paul, Demas had professed to look forward to the crown of righteousness that would never fade away. He had preached and proclaimed that he was longing for the age to come and the return of the Lord Jesus Christ (2 Timothy 4:8). But now he was turning his back on the crown of righteousness and, instead of loving Christ's appearing, he had fallen in love with this present age.

Perhaps the world had come to him in the guises most suited to the desires lying latent in his heart. He had begun to feel the strings of his heart being tugged towards the pleasures of this age. His grip on the age to come had been released, he had fallen back into the embraces of this age and he had gone to Thessalonica.

As a pastor, Paul's heart was broken because he didn't know whether Demas had just backslidden or whether he had committed the final apostasy. Even now, we don't know the end of Demas' story. However, there is still hope and encouragement in these verses. For Demas is not the only name mentioned here; in verse 11, John Mark is mentioned. We might call him the Demas of Paul's earlier life. He deserted Paul (we can only guess why) but he was restored.

Here then is the message: there is restoration and forgiveness for returning deserters. In Christ, there is a welcome for people like Demas, people like you and me, when we return to the Lord in repentance and faith.

Do you feel the strings of your heart being tugged by the pleasures of this age? Can you sense yourself losing focus on the crown of righteousness and the age to come? Today, turn back to God. The restoration offered to John Mark and Demas is still available. God is ready and waiting to welcome you.

There is hope for the backslider. God especially describes his grace to backsliders in Hosea 14. God is so amazing! Even though our backsliding insults him, dishonors him, grieves him, and pushes away his love, still he calls us to return to him. This requires repentance: coming to grips with the badness of our sins against God and turning away from them to the Lord, with a firm resolution to follow his commands. It requires turning from our reliance on ourselves (and other mere men) and renewing our trust in Christ alone. Such trust does not use Christ as a means to get something you want, but rests in Christ as what you want above all else.

(Joel Beeke, 'Getting Back into the Race', 8 November 2011, <www.thegospelcoalition.org/article/getting-back-into-the-race>, accessed 6 January 2021)

Hebrews

We don't know who wrote the book of Hebrews, but we do know why it was written. In the face of persecution, some Jewish Christians were drifting away from the gospel. Unbelief had crept in; they were not making any spiritual progress and they had given up meeting together. Like the earlier generation of Israelites in the desert, they were in danger of facing God's judgment. The writer makes it clear that slipping back into the comfortable ways of Judaism was not an option because Christ's coming had changed the spiritual landscape for ever. Christ was God's full and final revelation; he completed Israel's history, law, ceremonial rituals and priesthood.

Hebrews urges believers to remain faithful, by pointing them to Christ's absolute supremacy in divine revelation and his absolute sufficiency in Christian experience: 'fix your thoughts . . . [and fix your] eyes on Jesus' (Hebrews 3:1; 12:2).

Day 21

Read Hebrews 3:1–6
Key verses: Hebrews 3:5–6

....

> [5] *'Moses was faithful as a servant in all God's house,'*
> *bearing witness to what would be spoken by God in*
> *the future.* [6] *But Christ is faithful as the Son over God's*
> *house. And we are his house, if indeed we hold firmly*
> *to our confidence and the hope in which we glory.*

What attributes of God should Christians share?

'Faithful' is one of the Bible's great descriptions of God towards us, and also of all those who are in Christ.

Paul speaks in Ephesians 1:1 of those who are 'faithful in Christ Jesus'. In his parable of the talents, Jesus speaks of the faithful and wise servants. Hebrews 11 is a catalogue of those who lived by faith, who were faithful in all the different circumstances of life. And Revelation 2:10 challenges us to 'Be faithful, even to the point of death', so that we may receive life as our 'victor's crown'.

Jesus is our supreme pattern of faithfulness, and we are to 'fix' our 'thoughts on' him (Hebrews 3:1). But we are also to consider Moses as a pattern of faithfulness (verse 2), a faithful servant of God (verse 5). He faced Pharaoh, led the Israelites across the Red Sea and remonstrated with the people about the golden calf.

It is easy to look over the fence and say, 'If only I were So-and-so. If only this hadn't happened to me . . .' But God has called you where you are, and it is there that he wants you to be faithful. Moses wouldn't have chosen the life of a leader of escapee slaves; he had been pretty comfortable in Egypt. But God called him to lead the Israelites, and he stands out through the whole Old Testament as the supreme example of faithfulness.

Christ was also a faithful servant to God (verse 2). But he was more than that. He was faithful as 'the Son over God's house' (verse 6). For the Jews who read this letter, there was no one who had ever walked closer to God than Moses. But the writer says, 'Yes, there is – Jesus!' Moses was part of the house, but Christ was the builder and therefore worthy of greater honour.

Like Christ, we are God's sons and daughters. We share the wonderful privilege of being members of the eternal family, as 'holy brothers and sisters, who share in the heavenly calling' (verse 1). And our faithfulness, our perseverance, is the evidence that we are children of God, part of God's household: 'We are his house, if indeed we hold firmly to our confidence and the hope in which we glory' (verse 6).

For the doubters, the drifters and the weary, the encouragement is to 'fix your thoughts on Jesus' (verse 1). Greater even than Moses, he is worthy of our trust and obedience. Through him, God built his household: a community of believers saved by faith in Christ's death on the cross. Jesus' faithfulness on the cross means that our salvation is secure – now and for eternity. Today, praise God for Jesus' faithfulness, which means that we can 'hold firmly to our confidence and the hope in which we glory'.

Day 22

Read Hebrews 3:7 – 4:13
Key verse: Hebrews 4:1

....

Therefore, since the promise of entering his rest still stands, let us be careful that none of you be found to have fallen short of it.

Most of us need the carrot-and-stick approach: encouragement to remain faithful but also warnings against complacency.

Here we have a warning – three symptoms of falling away – so that we can recognize and prevent unfaithfulness.

• *A hardening heart.* Hebrews 3:7–11 quotes Psalm 95, which refers to the Israelites' lack of faith after they had escaped from Egypt. Joshua and Caleb believed God's Word that Israel could enter the Promised Land, but the rest did not. This unbelief led to thirty-eight years of wandering in the desert because people hardened their hearts towards God's Word. How well do we listen to and obey God's Word?

- *A turning away.* A consequence of hardening our hearts is that we turn away from the living God. We develop 'sinful, unbelieving' hearts (Hebrews 3:12). If we don't want to hear God, we soon don't want to have contact with him. We stop reading the Bible, attending our small groups and, perhaps, eventually don't go to church at all. Our turning away progresses because we do not want to be convicted by the Word. Therefore, we avoid it.

  The Israelites quickly turned away from God while Moses was on the mountain receiving the Ten Commandments. In his absence, they fashioned a golden calf and had an orgy (3:16–18). Aaron's excuse was this: 'So I told them, "Whoever has any gold jewellery, take it off." Then they gave me the gold, and I threw it into the fire, and out came this calf!' (Exodus 32:24). Aaron and the Israelites were deceived by their sin. When we begin to turn away from God, we also deceive ourselves and shut our ears to the truth we know so well.

- *A falling away.* We believe that once we have turned to Christ, we have 'crossed over from death to life' (John 5:24) and that no one can snatch us from the Father's hand (John 10:28–29). We have eternal life, beginning now, and nothing can separate us from the love of God in Christ Jesus (Romans 8:38–39). But you can't negate the force of Hebrews 4:11: 'So let us do our best to enter that rest. But if we disobey God, as the people of Israel did, we will fall' (NLT). This message is written to Christians: beware, in case you fall away!

If you are so hardened that you feel you could never fall away, you are probably more likely to do so. But if you are humble before God as a sinner saved by grace, although still wrestling with the sinful nature within you, you will hold to the wonderful doctrine of the preservation of the saints. You'll never be complacent as you look at the sin that can easily deceive, even in a Christian.

Because God is faithful, the promise of entering into his eternal rest still stands. With such a glorious future ahead, don't give in to complacency. Rather, press on all the more in faithfulness. Keep your heart soft towards God: obey his Word; pray often; join with your church family for worship and service; and spur one another on.

I have chosen the way of faithfulness;
    I have set my heart on your laws.
(Psalm 119:30)

Day 23

Read Hebrews 3:7 – 4:13
Key verses: Hebrews 3:12–13

....

12 See to it, brothers and sisters, that none of you has a sinful, unbelieving heart that turns away from the living God. 13 But encourage one another daily, as long as it is called 'Today', so that none of you may be hardened by sin's deceitfulness.

How well does your church look after new Christians? What care and provision are in place? This stage after birth is most important. We must invest in new believers for weeks and months, as what God has begun in them grows and takes root.

The writer to the Hebrews gives us four vital measures to put in place for ourselves and in the lives of those starting out on their Christian journey. It is never too early to guard our wayward hearts. He explains that unfaithfulness is prevented by four things.

- *Examination (3:12).* The New International Version of the Bible says, 'See to it'; the English Standard Version says, 'Take care'. Self-examination is required. Will you stop and review your life? Will you ask yourself straight questions about where you are before God? Give yourself a spiritual check-up and say to God, 'Have I slipped up? Have I gone forward? What do you want to say to me?'

- *Encouragement (3:13).* Have you encouraged someone today with a comment, a note or a text? Each of us has a ministry of encouraging the good, true and positive things in other Christians. Sin deceives us and Satan is seeking to destroy us, but encouragement from another Christian can strengthen us against temptation. Each morning, ask God, 'Whom can I encourage today?'

- *Effort (4:11).* The writer is talking about the effort of learning, thinking, training, developing and applying the faith, moving towards a greater maturity and usefulness for God. Never stop wanting to learn more about the Lord. We must keep making this God-blessed effort because we have to look to 'him to whom we must give account' (4:13).

- *Exposure (4:12–13).* Scripture is described as a double-edged sword, a short dagger, like a surgeon's knife that gets into where the problem is. It is 'living and active'; it is made personally alive to us by the Holy Spirit's action. It 'penetrates' us, reaching the deep recesses of the heart, and our inmost thoughts, subconscious motives and hidden agendas. 'It judges the thoughts and attitudes of the heart.' The Greek word for 'judges' here is one used in wrestling. God's Word grabs you, overthrows you just like a wrestler. Will you spend time reading and studying God's Word, letting it do its work in your heart?

There is nothing mystical about faithfulness. It is not a fluke, but the result of grace-driven effort.

Apart from grace-driven effort, people do not gravitate toward godliness, prayer, obedience to Scripture, faith and delight in the Lord. We drift toward compromise and call it tolerance; we drift toward disobedience and call it freedom; we drift toward superstition and call it faith. We cherish the indiscipline of lost self-control and call it relaxation; we slouch toward prayerlessness and delude ourselves into thinking we have escaped legalism; we slide toward godlessness and convince ourselves we have been liberated.

(D. A. Carson, *For the Love of God*, vol. 2, IVP, 2011, 23 January)

Day 24

Read Hebrews 4:14 – 5:6
Key verses: Hebrews 4:14–16

. . . .

14 Therefore, since we have a great high priest who has ascended into heaven, Jesus the Son of God, let us hold firmly to the faith we profess. 15 For we do not have a high priest who is unable to feel sympathy for our weaknesses, but we have one who has been tempted in every way, just as we are – yet he did not sin. 16 Let us then approach God's throne of grace with confidence, so that we may receive mercy and find grace to help us in our time of need.

Are you a confident person?

Whatever your personality, there are two things that the writer to the Hebrews urges us to do confidently that will build and establish our faithfulness: to hold firmly to the faith we profess and approach the throne of grace.

- *Let us hold firmly to the faith we profess.* Many people today are scathing of Christianity. We, however, can be confident because our faith rests not on human philosophy but in Christ, the Son of God. He is already triumphant in resurrection and ascension; he is the King of kings. What is more, this faith works. We can look around and see evidence of how the gospel message transforms lives.

- *Let us approach God's throne of grace.* Don't just stand there, saying, 'Isn't it marvellous?' Be confident about this privilege and use it. Before Jesus' death, the way to approach God was via the tabernacle, the temple and through a high priest. But the cross changed all that, and it was a game-changer for first-century Jews. A revolution had taken place: the temple curtain had been torn in two and the way into the holy of holies had been opened by the blood of Jesus. We must use this privilege to approach God's throne of grace directly, so that we may receive mercy and also find grace in time of need.

  And when you come to his throne, come honestly and openly, as you are. Nothing is hidden from God's sight, so don't hold anything back as if he can't see the recesses of your life. Come because Jesus shared in our humanity and has 'sympathy'. The Greek word used here is found only in the New Testament; it means to 'suffer with'. Jesus has understood our temptation; therefore we can come before God knowing that he understands.

We can hold on tightly to the faith and come into God's presence because of Jesus' faithfulness as God's Son and as our high priest. Living as a Christian is not a matter of crossing our fingers and hoping everything will work out in the end. Our faithfulness is not dependent on human wisdom, favourable circumstances or how confident we feel, but on the character and work of Jesus Christ.

Today, use the privilege Christ bought for you on the cross and approach God's throne with confidence. While conscious of his presence, meditate on Christ's character, tell yourself the gospel message, receive mercy and grace, and ask for help to press on and hold fast.

Day 25

Read Hebrews 6:11–20
Key verses: Hebrews 6:17–18

· ·

[17] Because God wanted to make the unchanging nature of his purpose very clear to the heirs of what was promised, he confirmed it with an oath. [18] God did this so that, by two unchangeable things in which it is impossible for God to lie, we who have fled to take hold of the hope set before us may be greatly encouraged.

Who is the most faithful believer you know?

The writer of Hebrews presents Abraham as an example of one who had 'faith and patience' (Hebrews 6:12). He left his home believing God's promise that he would give him a new land, make him into a great nation and bless him (Genesis 12). Many years later, his wife gave birth to Isaac, whom, Abraham was told, was the heir of the promise. In Genesis 22:2, God says to Abraham, 'Take your son, your only son whom you love . . . Sacrifice him.'

Abraham knows that it is through his son that the promise will come, but he obeys God, reasoning that God can bring Isaac back from the dead (Hebrews 11:19). And so, Abraham draws the knife, holds it high and is about to sacrifice his beloved son. Then a voice says:

> Do not lay a hand on the boy . . . because you have not withheld from me your son, your only son . . . I swear by myself, declares the LORD, that . . . I will surely bless you and make your descendants as numerous as the stars in the sky and as the sand on the seashore . . . through your offspring all nations on earth will be blessed, because you have obeyed me.
> (Genesis 22:12, 16–18)

God has already promised, but now he swears on oath that he will bless all nations through this son. In a court of law, you might say, 'I swear by almighty God that the evidence I shall give shall be the truth, the whole truth and nothing but the truth.' To swear an oath is to say that if I lie, God may deal with me ever so severely. But why does God swear? Is his promise not enough?

God's promise is certain; he does not lie. But here he makes his purpose to bless doubly clear. He didn't swear for Abraham's sake: Abraham already trusted the promise, and he had been willing to offer up his own son. But it's for us – the heirs of the promise – so that, by the promise and the oath, we have a double assurance: 'God did this so that we who have fled to take hold of the hope before us may be greatly encouraged' (Hebrews 6:18).

If you are feeling lazy and sluggish in your Christian life (verses 11–12), if you are tempted to let your relationship with Jesus slip, remember the promise and oath of God and be 'greatly encouraged'. He does not lie; he cannot break his oath; he cannot break his promise – he is completely trustworthy.

Jesus' death and resurrection are the proof that any promise God has ever made, he keeps (2 Corinthians 1:20). We can bank our eternity on the promises of God. Today, be 'greatly encouraged' by the faithfulness of God. Because he is faithful in his character, and therefore faithful to his promises and purposes, we can trust him completely – now and for eternity.

Day 26

Read Hebrews 6:11–20
Key verses: Hebrews 6:19–20

. . . .

[19]We have this hope as an anchor for the soul, firm and secure. It enters the inner sanctuary behind the curtain, [20]where our forerunner, Jesus, has entered on our behalf. He has become a high priest for ever, in the order of Melchizedek.

How do we make sure that we don't drift away from Christ?

We have seen from a variety of Bible passages that effort is required on our part. The writer to the Hebrews underlines this:

We want each of you to show this same diligence to the very end, so that what you hope for may be fully realized. We do not want you to become lazy, but to imitate those who through faith and patience inherit what has been promised.
(Hebrews 6:11–12)

However, the great encouragement in these verses is that we have an anchor that will hold us fast. We have 'an anchor for the soul' that is 'firm and secure' (verse 19). Anchors bury themselves in the bed of the sea to make sure that the ship doesn't move. But, in an unusual feat of geography and gravity, this 'anchor' goes up, rather than down. It's as if it's whirled above the head and launched into the heavens, into the sky, into the holy of holies, the throne room of God, the very place where God himself dwells.

The promise of God comes from heaven to Abraham. It is fulfilled in Jesus Christ, in his death and resurrection, and then he returns through the curtain, into the presence of God, where he goes before us. He is the forerunner, opening the way for us to follow. The Lord Jesus Christ is an anchor, the promise of our sure and certain hope of an eternal inheritance. This is God's unchangeable and unstoppable promise to bless his people, that we might be eternally secure.

Think of a ship in a storm, tossed and thrown about, drifting, in real danger of hitting the rocks. That is what life is like if we let go of the anchor, if we let go of Christ, if we let go of his promise. Now, imagine being in that storm as you drop anchor. It's still choppy; you still go up and down; the storm may still cause you to be seasick.

But you are safe and secure. You will not hit the rocks as long as that anchor is secure.

Perhaps you find yourself under pressure from circumstances. It could be that you feel alone and fearful. You might find yourself saying, 'I'm not sure if I can keep going with Christ.' God's Word says, 'You have an anchor for your soul – Christ.' Cling to him – devote yourself to prayer, grow in your relationship with him through God's Word, obey him through the power of the Holy Spirit – and he will hold you fast.

Jesus' faithfulness is our anchor. Nothing, or no one else, can offer the security our souls crave. As our forerunner, Jesus blazed a trail for us into the presence of God; as our high priest, he offered the perfect sacrifice of himself at Calvary. Now he sits at the right hand of God praying for us (Romans 8:34). Whatever storms you face today, remember, you have an anchor that cannot fail – Christ himself.

Revelation

As early as the end of the first century, the future of the church hung in the balance. False teaching and internal division were rife. Domitian, the Roman emperor, had instigated persecution against those who would not worship him as lord. The apostle John, exiled on the island of Patmos, wrote to encourage believers to resist the demands of the emperor. He exhorted them to stand firm against the devil's schemes and to look forward to Christ's triumphant return, which would ensure their complete vindication.

The book of Revelation is full of amazing visions and is highly symbolic. We won't understand every detail, but the call to faithfulness comes across loudly and clearly. Christ's message is to resist compromising our faith and to stand firm in trials, because he will return soon and our faithfulness will be rewarded.

Day 27

Read Revelation 2:18–29
Key verse: Revelation 2:20

....

I have this against you: you tolerate that woman Jezebel, who calls herself a prophet. By her teaching she misleads my servants into sexual immorality and the eating of food sacrificed to idols.

Do your words and worship on Sunday match your behaviour and values on Monday?

Jesus saw the love, faith, service and perseverance of the church at Thyatira (Revelation 2:19), but he also called them out on their compromise.

The city's commerce was operated by trade guilds. If you wanted to progress, you had to network in these guilds. But their meetings involved offering food to idols and emperor worship. What should Christians do? It seems that a prophetess in the church was saying, 'It's not a big deal. On Sunday, pledge allegiance to Jesus as Lord. On Monday, say that Caesar is lord.'

But the risen Christ calls this compromise spiritual adultery.

'Immorality' (verse 20) may refer to immoral acts in pagan rituals but, usually, in the book of Revelation, it refers to spiritual adultery (see Revelation 17:1–2; 18:1–3; 19:1–2). That's why Jesus calls this prophetess Jezebel. Jezebel was the foreign-born queen who had married the Israelite king Ahab. She had introduced the worship of Baal alongside the worship of the Lord (see 1 and 2 Kings). The Israelites didn't abandon worshipping the Lord to worship Baal; instead, they bowed to the two side by side. In the same way, the Jezebel of Thyatira was not *outside* the church; she was *inside* the church, worshipping Jesus on Sunday but also, on Monday morning, worshipping other gods.

How about us? Do we have two sets of values? On Sunday, do we believe God's Word as it speaks of Jesus Christ and yet, on Monday, give credence to the adverts that say life, identity and fulfilment are found through what we can buy? On Sunday, do we trust our future to the sovereign Lord but, on Monday, trust our future to the bank?

We can sympathize with Jezebel. After all, how can we prosper in the workplace, how will we find a marriage partner, unless we are prepared to compromise a bit? But Jesus says that the prophetess 'misleads' her servants. The Greek word for 'misleads' is one that is used in Revelation only of Satan, his false prophet and Babylon the Prostitute (Revelation 12:9; 13:14; 18:23; 20:3, 8, 10). Ultimately, compromise led to judgment for Jezebel and her followers (Revelation 2:22–23).

Christ will not tolerate spiritual adultery. When addressing the church, he opens with 'These are the words of the Son of God' (verse 18). Caesar was called a son of god or a son of Zeus. The Son of God challenges these claims head on. There can be no accommodation between Christ and Caesar, between Christ and the world.

Today, the risen Christ, the Son of God, sets his eyes 'like blazing fire' (Revelation 2:18) on our lives. He sees our love, faith, service and perseverance. But, jealous for our wholehearted devotion, he also wants to expose any spiritual adultery. Do your conversations at home, your behaviour at work and your bank balance reflect your trust in God and in his Word or do they mirror the concerns and priorities of the world? Ask God to reveal your areas of compromise and give you strength to be as faithful to God's will as Jesus was.

Day 28

Read Revelation 2:18–29
Key verse: Revelation 2:23

....

Then all the churches will know that I am he who searches hearts and minds, and I will repay each of you according to your deeds.

Worldliness is whatever makes sin look normal and right-eousness look strange.
(Kevin DeYoung, *The Hole in Our Holiness,* Crossway, 2012, p. 37)

It would be very easy to define worldliness in terms of activities that Christians shouldn't do and places that they shouldn't go. But the risen Lord has eyes 'like blazing fire' (Revelation 2:18) and he is looking at our hearts because that is where the true battle for faithful, holy living takes place.

There are Christians leading respectable lives with exemplary behaviour who are losing the battle for the heart.

Their actions arise from duty instead of grace, and they act out of self-righteousness instead of glory for God. Verse 23 is a quote from Jeremiah 17:

> The heart is deceitful above all things
>> and beyond cure.
>> Who can understand it?

And the answer comes:

> 'I the LORD search the heart
>> and examine the mind,
> to reward each person according to their conduct,
>> according to what their deeds deserve.'
> (Jeremiah 17:9–10)

In Jeremiah 17:5–8, the Lord explains why the heart is so important. Adversity, trials, suffering and problems will come to us all. What makes the difference is how our hearts respond. If our hearts turn away from the Lord when the heat comes, we will be like a bush in the desert (verse 6). But if we trust in the Lord, we will be like a tree planted by water (verse 8).

The key to holy living is not circumstances but a heart that trusts the Lord:

> Teach me your way, LORD,
>> that I may rely on your faithfulness;

> give me an undivided heart,
> > that I may fear your name.
> (Psalm 86:11)

Elsewhere, the psalmist speaks of a fixed heart and a heart that is steadfast. We live at a time when people change their sets of values in different contexts. The challenge for believers is to have hearts that are fixed on faithfully serving Jesus.

And we are in this together. Holiness is a community project. This is how the writer to the Hebrews puts it:

> See to it, brothers and sisters, that none of you has a sinful, unbelieving heart that turns away from the living God. But encourage one another daily, as long as it is called 'Today', so that none of you may be hardened by sin's deceitfulness.
> (Hebrews 3:12–13)

Outwardly, you may look holy – you go to church, help with Sunday school and serve on rotas. But true holiness is a matter of the heart – it is being faithful to God when no one is watching, faithful when your circumstances are difficult and faithfully obedient in the little things.

Holiness is the sum of a million little things – the avoidance of little evils and little foibles, the setting aside of little bits of worldliness and little acts of compromise, the putting to death of little inconsistencies and little indiscretions, the attention to little duties and little dealings, the hard work of little self-denials and little self-restraints, the cultivation of little benevolences and little forbearances.

(Kevin DeYoung, *The Hole in our Holiness*, Crossway, 2012, p. 145)

Day 29

Read Revelation 2:18–29
Key verses: Revelation 2:24–25

....

> [24] *Now I say to the rest of you in Thyatira, to you who do not hold to her teaching and have not learned Satan's so-called deep secrets, 'I will not impose any other burden on you,* [25] *except to hold on to what you have until I come.'*

'Hold on!' That is Jesus' command.

The risen Christ commends the church at Thyatira for not following the 'deep secrets'. Verse 24 may be ironic; it may be that Jezebel talked about the deep secrets of God, and Christ says that they are really the deep secrets of Satan. Or it may be that Jezebel's followers claimed to follow the way of Satan so that they could take part in pagan rituals without being affected.

Either way, the point is that Jesus rejects so-called deep things. We already have the wisdom and power of God in the message of Christ crucified. There is no higher way, no special teaching, no advanced message. The secret of holiness is no secret at all; it is to hold on to the gospel, goodness, grace and sovereignty of God.

That doesn't mean it is easy; it's still a battle. Behind every sin is a lie, a false promise. The battle for holiness is a battle to believe the truth, the truth that only God can bring true joy and justify us through his grace. But don't think of this battle for holiness as some kind of dreary struggle in which you have to give up pleasure. It's not! It is a battle to delight in God. 'The fight of faith is the fight to keep your heart content in Christ, to really believe and keep on believing that he will meet every need and satisfy every longing' (John Piper, *Future Grace*, Multnomah Press, 2012, p. 222).

When we can't see God's hand or feel his love, and his return seems very far away, it is a struggle to hold on to gospel truths. In our battle-weary moments, the happiness that the world offers – money, sex and personal satisfaction – seems very tempting. But these are precisely the times not to lose our grip on the gospel but to hold on even tighter, to ask God to strengthen us to delight in his truth, so that we remain faithful till the end.

We . . . thank God for you, brothers and sisters loved by the Lord, because God chose you as firstfruits to be saved through the sanctifying work of the Spirit and through belief in the truth. He called you to this through our gospel, that you might share in the glory of our Lord Jesus Christ.

So then, brothers and sisters, stand firm and hold fast to the teachings we passed on to you, whether by word of mouth or by letter.

May our Lord Jesus Christ himself and God our Father, who loved us and by his grace gave us eternal encouragement and good hope, encourage your hearts and strengthen you in every good deed and word.

(2 Thessalonians 2:13–17)

Day 30

Read Revelation 2:18–29

Key verses: Revelation 2:26–28

....

> [26] *To the one who is victorious and does my will to the end, I will give authority over the nations –* [27] *that one 'will rule them with an iron sceptre and will dash them to pieces like pottery' – just as I have received authority from my Father.* [28] *I will also give that one the morning star.*

What motivates you to remain faithful?

The promise of rewards can encourage us all. In these verses, John gives us a vision of the future in which Christians are victorious and have authority. The morning star is the planet Venus, a Roman symbol of victory. The generals erected temples to the goddess Venus and carried her symbols on their standards. But look closely, because the risen Christ turns our ideas of success and victory upside down. Verse 27 is a quote from Psalm 2 and, in that psalm, God gives his Son authority over the nations. Now Jesus says that he is giving that authority to his people. In the Great Commission, Jesus sends us, with his authority, to teach the nations to obey his commands (Matthew 28:18–20). We exercise authority over the nations through the Word of God.

The same words from Psalm 2 are quoted in Revelation 12:11, where we are told what it means to overcome:

> They triumphed . . .
>> by the blood of the Lamb
>> and by the word of their testimony;
> they did not love their lives so much
>> as to shrink from death.

How do we overcome? How do we exercise authority? By the blood of the Lamb. God revolutionizes our criteria for success: we rule by serving; we conquer by loving; we overcome by suffering.

And our greatest reward, our ultimate success, will be to receive the morning star (verse 28). In Revelation 22:16, Jesus says that he is the 'Morning Star'. The star is seen in the sky just before dawn. Jesus tells us that he himself is the sign of a new day. He is assuring us that we will be part of God's new dawn, God's new age. We will see God's kingdom, share in his banquet and, on that day, we will see Jesus.

The Christians in Thyatira had to choose between success in life and remaining faithful to God. It's the decision that we all have to make between worldliness and holiness. As we face that choice, Jesus is raising our sights. Faithfulness might mean suffering and hardship in this life, but beyond that is the dawn of a world made new, in which God dwells with his people.

One day soon, the morning star will appear. On that great day, all God's promises will be fully and finally realized, and we will receive the reward for our faithfulness – the Lord Jesus himself. As we wait for the return of Christ and his unveiling of the new heavens and new earth, persevere a little while longer. In the darkness before that glorious new dawn, keep choosing faithfulness to Christ over success in this life – whatever the cost – knowing that, very soon, we will be with Jesus, enjoying him for ever.

For further study

If you would like to read more on the theme of faithfulness, you might find this selection of books helpful.

Books on the theme of staying faithful to God for the long haul:

- Christopher Ash, *Zeal without Burnout: Seven keys to a lifelong ministry of sustainable sacrifice* (The Good Book Company, 2016).

- Paul Mallard, *Staying Fresh: Serving with joy* (IVP, 2015).

- Trillia J. Newbell, *Sacred Endurance: Finding grace and strength for a lasting faith* (IVP, 2019).

Biographies of faithful men and women to inspire and encourage your own spiritual journey:

- John Piper, *21 Servants of Sovereign Joy: Faithful, flawed, and fruitful* (Crossway, 2018).

- Noël Piper, *Faithful Women and Their Extraordinary God* (Crossway, 2005).

- Dr Helen Roseveare, *Living Faith: Willing to be stirred as a pot of paint* (Christian Focus, 2007).

Books on the theme of staying faithful to the gospel while engaging with culture:

- Timothy Keller and John Inazu, *Uncommon Ground: Living faithfully in a world of difference* (Thomas Nelson, 2020).

- Rebecca Manley Pippert, *Stay Salt: The world has changed – our message must not* (The Good Book Company, 2020).

Keswick Ministries

Our purpose

Keswick Ministries exists to inspire and equip Christians to love and live for Christ in his world.

God's purpose is to bring his blessing to all the nations of the world (Genesis 12:3). That promise of blessing, which touches every aspect of human life, is ultimately fulfilled through the life, death, resurrection, ascension and future return of Christ. All the people of God are called to participate in his missionary purposes, wherever he may place them. The central vision of Keswick Ministries is to see the people of God equipped, inspired and refreshed to fulfil that calling, directed and guided by God's Word in the power of his Spirit, for the glory of his Son.

Our priorities

There are three fundamental priorities which shape all that we do as we look to serve the local church.

- *Hearing God's Word*: the Scriptures are the foundation for the church's life, growth and mission, and Keswick Ministries is committed to preach and teach God's

Word in a way that is faithful to Scripture and relevant to Christians of all ages and backgrounds.

- *Becoming like God's Son*: from its earliest days, the Keswick movement has encouraged Christians to live godly lives in the power of the Spirit, to grow in Christ-likeness and to live under his Lordship in every area of life. This is God's will for his people in every culture and generation.

- *Serving God's mission*: the authentic response to God's Word is obedience to his mission, and the inevitable result of Christlikeness is sacrificial service. Keswick Ministries seeks to encourage committed discipleship in family life, work and society, and energetic engagement in the cause of world mission.

Our ministry

- *Keswick Convention*. The Convention attracts some 12,000 to 15,000 Christians from the UK and around the world to Keswick every summer. It provides Bible teaching for all ages, vibrant worship, a sense of unity across generations and denominations, and an inspirational call to serve Christ in the world. It caters for children of all ages and has a strong youth and young adult programme. And it all takes place in the beautiful

Lake District – a perfect setting for rest, recreation and refreshment.

- *Keswick fellowship*. For more than 140 years, the work of Keswick has affected churches worldwide, not just through individuals being changed but also through Bible conventions that originate or draw their inspiration from the Keswick Convention. Today, there is a network of events that share Keswick Ministries' priorities across the UK and in many parts of Europe, Asia, North America, Australia, Africa and the Caribbean. Keswick Ministries is committed to strengthening the network in the UK and beyond through prayer, news and co-operative activity.

- *Keswick teaching and training*. Keswick Ministries is developing a range of inspiring, Bible-centred teaching and training that focuses on equipping believers for 'whole-of-life' discipleship. This builds on the same concern that started the Convention, that all Christians live godly lives in the power of the Spirit in all spheres of life in God's world. Some of the smaller and more intensive events focus on equipping attendees, while others focus on inspiring them. Some are for pastors, others for those in different forms of church leadership, while many are for any Christian. The aim of all the courses is for the participants to return home refreshed to serve.

- *Keswick resources*. Keswick Ministries produces a range of books, devotionals, study guides and digital resources to inspire and equip the church to live for Christ. The printed resources focus on the core foundations of Christian life and mission, and help the people of God in their walk with Christ. The digital resources make teaching and sung worship from the Keswick Convention available in a variety of ways.

Our unity

The Keswick movement worldwide has adopted a key Pauline statement to describe its gospel inclusivity: 'All one in Christ Jesus' (Galatians 3:28). Keswick Ministries works with evangelicals from a wide variety of church backgrounds, on the understanding that they share a commitment to the essential truths of the Christian faith as set out in our statement of belief.

Our contact details

T: 017687 80075
E: info@keswickministries.org
W: www.keswickministries.org
Mail: Keswick Ministries, Rawnsley Centre, Main Street, Keswick, Cumbria CA12 5NP, England

Related titles from IVP

Food for the Journey

The Food for the Journey series offers daily devotionals from much loved Bible teachers at the Keswick Convention in an ideal pocket-sized format – to accompany you wherever you go.

Available in the series

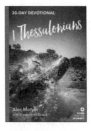

1 Thessalonians

Alec Motyer with Elizabeth McQuoid

978 1 78359 439 9

2 Timothy

Michael Baughen with Elizabeth McQuoid

978 1 78359 438 2

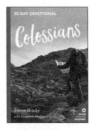

Colossians

Steve Brady with Elizabeth McQuoid

978 1 78359 722 2

Ezekiel

Liam Goligher with Elizabeth McQuoid

978 1 78359 603 4

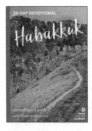

Habakkuk

Jonathan Lamb with Elizabeth McQuoid

978 1 78359 652 2

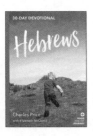

Hebrews

Charles Price with Elizabeth McQuoid

978 1 78359 611 9

James

Stuart Briscoe with Elizabeth McQuoid

978 1 78359 523 5

John 14 – 17

Simon Manchester with Elizabeth McQuoid

978 1 78359 495 5

Available from your local Christian bookshop or **www.ivpbooks.com**